UNPRECEDENTED AMBITIONS

The 14th Amendment's Battle to Bar Trump from the Presidency

Timothy M. Mock

TABLE OF CONTENTS

Introduction: The Controversy of Presidential Eligibility

Chapter 1: The Origins of the 14th Amendment

1.1 The Reconstruction Era

1.2 Birthright Citizenship: A Contested Principle

1.3 Equal Protection Clause

Chapter 2: Trump's Actions and the January 6 Attack

2.1 Events Leading to January 6

2.2 The Capitol Insurrection

2.3 Legal Definitions of Insurrection

Chapter 3: Legal Experts and Political Opinions

3.1 Debates among Legal Scholars

3.2 Political Perspectives

3.3 Public Reactions

Chapter 4: The Supreme Court's Role

Chapter 5: The Role of Key State Officials

5.1 Perspectives of State Secretaries of State

Conclusion: The Legacy of the 14th Amendment's Application

<u>**Introduction: The Controversy of Presidential Eligibility**</u>

In the wake of the tumultuous events of January 6th, a question emerged that challenged the very foundations of American democracy: Could Donald Trump, former President of the United States, be disqualified from running for a second term under the 14th Amendment? This amendment, a pillar of the nation's constitution, prohibits any public official who engaged in insurrection or rebellion against the United States from holding office.

It was Representative Jamie Raskin, a former constitutional law professor, who cast a spotlight on this issue just six weeks after the storming of the Capitol. He pointed out that Trump, by all appearances, fell squarely within the ambit of this constitutional prohibition, given his actions and rhetoric. The lawmakers who crafted the 14th Amendment in the aftermath of the Civil

War had individuals like Trump in mind when they penned these words.

Fast forward more than two years, and the conversation around the 14th Amendment has intensified. Trump now faces criminal charges related to his post-election efforts, heightening the scrutiny of his eligibility. In a surprising move, Trump addressed this constitutional provision, which had largely remained untouched in his public discourse, through his social media platform. His words echoed with defiance:

"Almost all legal scholars have voiced opinions that the 14th Amendment has no legal basis or standing relative to the upcoming 2024 Presidential Election. Like Election Interference, it is just another 'trick' being used by the Radical Left Communists, Marxists, and Fascists...."

However, beneath the surface, several intriguing aspects deserve our attention. Trump's choice of words, perhaps not entirely his own, diverged from his typical communication style. Moreover, his assertion that "almost all legal scholars" share his perspective directly contradicts prominent voices in the legal community who argue the opposite.

Two conservative legal scholars, in particular, have presented a compelling case that Trump is constitutionally ineligible to return to the White House. Their argument challenges Trump's continued influence on American democracy. Meanwhile, leading Democrats have also lent credence to the notion that Trump may have disqualified himself from future presidential runs, raising serious questions.

The path forward in determining Trump's eligibility is multi-faceted. Advocacy groups and concerned citizens have explored two major routes: urging state election authorities to rule against Trump's candidacy and challenging his eligibility through state election board complaints and lawsuits. These developments, with a focus on state primary ballots, promise to be pivotal in shaping the political landscape leading up to the 2024 election.

In this exploration of the 14th Amendment's potential to reshape the course of American politics, we delve into the historical origins, legal debates, and the evolving landscape of Trump's eligibility for the highest office in the land. Join us on this riveting journey through constitutional intricacies, political maneuvers, and the enduring questions surrounding democracy's resilience in the face of unprecedented challenges.

Chapter 1: The Origins of the 14th Amendment

In the turbulent aftermath of the American Civil War, the nation stood at a crossroads. The wounds of the conflict were deep, and the urgent need to address the status of newly emancipated slaves and the reintegration of Confederate states into the Union loomed large. It was against this backdrop that the 14th Amendment was conceived—a transformative addition to the United States Constitution. This pivotal amendment, ratified in 1868, emerged as a cornerstone of civil rights and equality in the country. To understand its significance and the debates surrounding its application to a figure like Donald Trump, we must first delve into the historical context and motivations behind its creation. In this chapter, we will explore the Reconstruction Era, the birthright citizenship principle, and the Equal Protection Clause, laying a solid foundation for the subchapters that follow.

1.1 The Reconstruction Era

The Reconstruction Era stands as a pivotal period in American history, marking a turbulent and transformative time in the aftermath of the Civil War. Emerging from the ashes of a nation divided, the United States faced the monumental task of rebuilding, both physically and politically.

A Nation in Turmoil

The Civil War, which raged from 1861 to 1865, had left the country deeply scarred. Cities lay in ruins, and the death toll had been staggering, with over 600,000 lives lost. More than just a military conflict, the war had been a clash of ideals and a struggle for the soul of the nation. The defeat of the Confederate States of America meant the end of slavery, but it did not automatically usher in a new era of racial equality and civil rights.

The Promise of Reconstruction

As the war concluded, a new chapter in American history began: Reconstruction. This was a period of immense promise and profound uncertainty. The promise lay in the opportunity to reimagine the South and the entire nation as a place where liberty and justice were truly for all. The uncertainty stemmed from the immense challenges of this endeavor, including the need to heal a divided nation and redefine the rights and status of formerly enslaved individuals.

The Three Reconstruction Amendments

Central to the Reconstruction effort were the three Reconstruction Amendments: the 13th, 14th, and 15th Amendments. These constitutional changes sought to eradicate the vestiges of slavery, secure civil rights, and establish suffrage for Black Americans. In this subchapter, our focus is on the 14th Amendment, which has become a cornerstone in the ongoing discussions about presidential eligibility, particularly in the case of Donald Trump.

The 14th Amendment: A Beacon of Equality

Ratified in 1868, the 14th Amendment was a beacon of hope for a nation grappling with its past and uncertain about its future. Its first section contains the Citizenship Clause, which declared that all persons born or naturalized in the United States were citizens, overturning the infamous Dred Scott v. Sandford decision of 1857. This clause established the principle of birthright citizenship, which remains a contentious issue in contemporary political debates.

Equal Protection Under the Law

Equally significant was the Equal Protection Clause of the 14th Amendment, which proclaimed that no state could "deny to any person within its jurisdiction the equal protection of the laws." This clause was a response to the deeply entrenched racism and discrimination that persisted in the post-war South and, to some extent, in the North as well. It aimed to secure equal rights for all, regardless of race or color.

The Reconstruction Era Unveiled

As we explore the Reconstruction Era in the context of the 14th Amendment, we will uncover the aspirations, challenges, and political maneuvering of this complex period. The struggles of that era, from the bitter battles over civil rights to the fervent debates in the halls of Congress, have a profound resonance today. The legacy of Reconstruction, particularly the 14th Amendment, continues to shape our understanding of citizenship, equality, and the constitutional rights of all Americans.

1.2 <u>Birthright Citizenship: A Contested Principle</u>

According to the 14th Amendment of the Bill of Rights, citizenship in the United States is now defined. It was ratified in 1868 in the aftermath of the Civil War to guarantee citizenship for all free African Americans, and it states: "All persons born or naturalized in the United States, and subject to the jurisdiction thereof, are citizens of the United States and of the State wherein they reside." When the Supreme Court heard the case of United States v. Wong Kim Ark in the late 1890s, the definition was put to the test. People born on American soil are treated as citizens in this situation, even if their parents are not.

However, if you go back roughly a century to the 1780s, the definition of American citizenship is less clear. Although they do not define citizenship in detail, the Constitution and the Bill of Rights both refer to it. Article I stipulates that to occupy legislative office, a person must be a citizen. No one may run for president unless they were a citizen of the United States at the time of the Constitution's adoption, according to Article II. Aware of what citizenship entailed, the Founders chose not to define it.

Outside of the Soil

A common, practical understanding of English common law—a legacy the nascent nation inherited from Great Britain—was something that federalists like Alexander Hamilton and anti-federalists like Patrick Henry shared when they were creating the Constitution, despite their disagreements on many other issues. Jus soli, a Latin phrase that means "right of the soil" or "birthright citizenship," was used under common law to define citizenship. In general, one was considered a British subject if they were born in the country. Jus soli became the "law of the land" for American citizens after the Founders applied this idea to their new form of government.

To the Blood's Right

In determining who was a citizen in the new country, the idea of jus sanguinis (Latin for "right of the blood") also came into play. According to this theory, citizenship was inherited from fathers to their offspring. "An act to establish a uniform Rule of Naturalization," approved by Congress in March 1790, declared that infants born to American men overseas or at sea were still regarded as "natural born citizens." No matter where they were born, the children would inherit the status of their fathers. The nations of Europe started employing jus sanguinis criteria to define citizenship in 1804, starting with France. This approach is being used today.

1.3 Equal Protection Clause

The University of North Carolina School of Law's Julius L. Chambers Distinguished Professor of Law and Director of the Center for Civil Rights

There is little question that the Equal Protection Clause was designed to prevent states from discriminating against blacks when it was ratified in 1868, immediately following the Civil War. However, the text of the Clause is quite vague and has diverged significantly from its original intent. For instance, despite the Clause's reference to "state[s]," it has been incorporated into the Fifth Amendment to prohibit discrimination by the federal government as well.

The Court debated whether racial segregation by the government violated the Constitution near the end of the eighteenth century. Did it count as discrimination if persons were put in various facilities based on race yet those facilities were supposedly equally suitable? In Plessy v. Ferguson (1896), the Supreme Court declared on a 7-1 vote that so-called "separate but equal" facilities (in that case, railway cars) for blacks and whites did not violate the Equal Protection Clause. Historians have argued about whether the Fourteenth Amendment was intended to eliminate such segregation. The ruling made racist laws from the Jim Crow era permanent. Justice John Marshall Harlan dissented, writing in a well-known dissent that "[o]ur Constitution is color-blind..." Until 1954, when it was overturned in Brown v. Board of Education, Plessy was the supreme law of the land. Separate schools for blacks and whites were declared illegal by the Supreme Court, which unanimously rejected the Plessy decision. In the protracted battle to end segregation that had been imposed by the government, not only in schools but also throughout American society, Brown marked a significant turning point. Brown was a turning moment, but the fight was far from over. For instance, the Supreme Court did not rule that laws forbidding interracial marriages were unconstitutional until Loving v. Virginia in 1967.

The Supreme Court has ruled that all racial discrimination, including that against whites, Hispanics, Asians, and Native Americans, is unconstitutional, despite the fact that the original intent of the law was to shield blacks from prejudice. These rulings have sparked a long-running discussion over the last few decades about whether it is lawful for governments to favor black, Hispanic, and Native American race in hiring, contracting, and university admissions. This issue will be covered in our individual statements.

The Equal Protection Clause has also been applied by the Supreme Court to forbid discrimination on grounds other than race. Most legislation are examined using what is referred to as "rational basis scrutiny." Here, any credible and legal justification for the discrimination is enough to make it legal. However, legislation that are based on alleged "suspect classifications" are given "heightened scrutiny." Here, the discrimination must be carefully crafted to serve the government's stated objectives and must be justified by significant or compelling factors. What classifications are considered "suspect"? It should come as no surprise that the categories of race and national origin are suspicious given the history of the

Equal Protection Clause. However, the Court has also ruled that classifications based on gender, immigration status, and marital status at birth are doubtful. Arguments that poverty and old age should be elevated to suspect category have been rejected by the Court.

Whether the Court should determine that sexual orientation is a suspect classification is one of the biggest debates now surrounding the Equal Protection Clause. The Supreme Court suggested that discrimination against homosexuals and lesbians can violate the Equal Protection Clause in its most recent ruling on same-sex marriage, Obergefell v. Hodges (2015). However, the Court did not make a decision regarding the appropriate level of scrutiny, leaving this issue for another time.

The Equal Protection Clause is a living, evolving document, like many other constitutional clauses.

Typical Interpretation

Study up on the 14th Amendment Podcast.

Is President Trump ineligible to hold office in accordance with the 14th Amendment?
Experts in constitutional law debate whether and how President Trump might be removed from office under Section 3 of the 14th Amendment.

Chapter 2: Trump's Actions and the January 6 Attack

In this pivotal chapter, we delve into the heart of the matter, exploring the intricate details surrounding Donald Trump's actions in the lead-up to and during the January 6, 2021 attack on the United States Capitol. This chapter serves as a comprehensive examination of the events that unfolded on that fateful day and the subsequent legal and political repercussions, all of which play a significant role in the broader conversation regarding the 14th Amendment and its potential impact on Trump's presidential eligibility.

2.1 Events Leading to January 6

In the annals of American history, few moments have been as fraught with tension and anticipation as the lead-up to January 6, 2021. This pivotal subchapter explores the multifaceted events and developments that set the stage for the unprecedented attack on the United States Capitol. To fully grasp the significance of January 6th, we must embark on a journey that traverses the final weeks of 2020 and the early days of the new year.

The 2020 Presidential Election

The story begins with the 2020 presidential election—an election held amid a global pandemic, intense political polarization, and an electorate deeply divided. Joe Biden, the Democratic nominee, faced off against the incumbent President, Donald Trump. The election process, with its unprecedented levels of mail-in voting, extended vote-counting periods, and pandemic-related challenges, laid the groundwork for an election that would be closely scrutinized and contested.

Trump's Refusal to Concede

As the nation watched with bated breath, Joe Biden was declared the winner of the election on

November 7, 2020. However, Donald Trump refused to concede, making unsubstantiated claims of widespread voter fraud and election rigging. This refusal to accept the election results ignited a political firestorm that would only intensify in the weeks to come.

Stop the Steal" Movement

Within days of the election, a movement emerged under the banner of "Stop the Steal." This movement, comprised of ardent Trump supporters and various right-wing activists, alleged that the election had been stolen from the President. Social media platforms became a breeding ground for these claims, with hashtags like #StopTheSteal spreading rapidly. It was within this online ecosystem that conspiracy theories and fervent beliefs took root.

Legal Challenges and State Certifications

In the wake of Trump's refusal to concede, a barrage of legal challenges descended upon the election results. Trump's legal team and allies launched numerous lawsuits in key battleground states, seeking to overturn the election results. These legal battles played out in courtrooms across the country, with the majority of them resulting in dismissals due to a lack of evidence.

Despite the legal setbacks, Trump's supporters held out hope that state legislatures would intervene to overturn the results. In some states, legislators considered these calls, but ultimately, the election results were certified, and the democratic process proceeded.

December 14: Electoral College Certification

One of the pivotal moments in the lead-up to January 6th occurred on December 14, 2020, when the Electoral College convened to certify the election results. In state capitals across the nation, electors cast their votes in accordance with the popular vote in their respective states. This process, a linchpin of the American electoral system, affirmed Joe Biden's victory, further diminishing the hopes of Trump and his supporters for a last-minute reversal of fortune.

Trump's Ongoing Refusal to Concede

Even after the Electoral College certification, President Trump continued to reject the legitimacy of the election. He intensified his rhetoric, insisting that the election had been "stolen" and that he was the rightful winner. Social media platforms, struggling to strike a balance between free speech and misinformation, faced a conundrum in how to handle the President's posts.

January 6, 2021: The Day of Reckoning

All eyes turned to January 6, 2021, as Congress convened in a joint session to certify the Electoral College results, a traditionally ceremonial event. Thousands of Trump supporters, fueled by the President's unyielding claims of election fraud, descended on

Washington, D.C. for a rally near the White House.

In the days leading up to January 6th, the United States found itself at a crossroads—a nation grappling with an unprecedented challenge to its democratic norms and processes. The events explored in this subchapter, from the election itself to the rise of the "Stop the Steal" movement, formed the backdrop against which the January 6th attack on the U.S. Capitol would unfold. The tension, rhetoric, and political divisions that characterized this period of American history would come to a head in a manner that would reverberate across the nation and the world.

2.2 The Capitol Insurrection

On January 6, 2021, the hallowed halls of the United States Capitol, a symbol of American democracy, became the scene of unprecedented chaos and violence. This subchapter delves into the shocking events that unfolded within the Capitol building on that fateful day, marking a dark moment in U.S. history.

Breaching the Citadel of Democracy

As Congress convened to certify the Electoral College results, the atmosphere was tense. Thousands of President Donald Trump's supporters had gathered in the nation's capital, responding to his call to "stop the steal." The rally near the White House had been charged with fervor, and many attendees believed they were answering the President's call to action.

The March to the Capitol

From the Ellipse, where Trump had addressed the crowd, many protesters began a march toward the Capitol. The President's speech, which included inflammatory rhetoric about "fighting like hell," seemed to embolden his supporters. As they reached the Capitol grounds, they encountered barricades and law enforcement personnel.

The Breach

Despite the security measures in place, the situation quickly escalated. Some in the crowd breached the barricades and stormed the Capitol building, shattering windows, and overwhelming the limited Capitol Police presence. The ensuing scenes were surreal and horrifying, as the mob made its way into the heart of American democracy.

Inside the Capitol

Once inside, the rioters roamed the halls of Congress, brandishing Confederate flags, Trump banners, and other symbols of their cause. Lawmakers and congressional staff were evacuated, while the mob occupied congressional chambers and offices. The certification of the Electoral College results, a fundamental aspect of the democratic process, was abruptly halted.

The Response of Law Enforcement

The breach of the Capitol exposed significant shortcomings in the security response. Despite ample warnings and intelligence suggesting potential violence, the initial response appeared unprepared for the scale of the attack. As the situation deteriorated, additional law enforcement agencies were deployed, and the National Guard was eventually called in to restore order.

Violence and Casualties

The chaos inside the Capitol resulted in multiple casualties. Several individuals died, including Capitol Police Officer Brian Sicknick, who succumbed to injuries sustained during the melee. Dozens of officers and protesters were injured, and the toll on the nation's psyche was immeasurable.

Evacuation of Elected Officials

Amid the violence, lawmakers and Vice President Mike Pence were evacuated to secure locations. The scenes of elected officials, in gas masks and sheltering from the mob, were a stark illustration of the gravity of the situation. The certification process was ultimately resumed and completed, solidifying Joe Biden's victory.

The Fallout and Condemnation

The events of January 6th sent shockwaves across the nation and the world. Leaders from both political parties condemned the attack on democracy. President Trump, after initial reluctance, issued a video statement urging his supporters to go home, but he continued to assert that the election was stolen from him

The breach of the Capitol on January 6, 2021, will forever be etched in the annals of American history. The images of that day—a mob occupying the halls of Congress, violence and chaos, the suspension of a fundamental democratic process—serve as a stark reminder of the fragility of democracy and the enduring consequences of political division. The events of that day set the stage for a cascade of legal and political repercussions, the consequences of which continue to shape the national discourse, including discussions about the potential application of the 14th Amendment to presidential eligibility.

2.3 Legal Definitions of Insurrection

To understand the gravity of the events that transpired on January 6, 2021, and their potential implications under the 14th Amendment, it is essential to explore the legal definitions of insurrection. These definitions, grounded in U.S. law and history, provide context for evaluating whether the actions of the mob that breached the Capitol amounted to insurrection or rebellion.

Insurrection Defined

Legally, insurrection refers to a violent uprising against the authority of a government or its officers. It is a term deeply rooted in the history of the United States, particularly during the Civil War and Reconstruction Era, when the nation grappled with issues of secession and rebellion.

Rebellion and Sedition

Rebellion and sedition are related concepts often associated with insurrection. Rebellion generally involves an organized and often armed resistance to established authority, with the intent to overthrow or oppose the government. Sedition, on the other hand, pertains to actions or speech inciting others to engage in rebellion or insurrection.

The 14th Amendment's Language

The 14th Amendment's relevance to the events of January 6th lies in its language, particularly in Section 3, which states that no person shall hold office if they have engaged in insurrection or rebellion against the United States or have given aid and comfort to its enemies.

Historical Precedents

To establish whether the Capitol breach constituted insurrection, it is instructive to examine historical precedents. The American Civil War, marked by secession and rebellion by Confederate states, serves as a defining period in U.S. history where the concept of insurrection played a central role.

The Whiskey Rebellion

Another notable historical example is the Whiskey Rebellion of 1791-1794. In response to a federal excise tax on whiskey, some farmers in western Pennsylvania staged violent protests and resisted the enforcement of the tax. President George Washington's decision to mobilize a militia to suppress the rebellion set a precedent for the federal government's authority to quell domestic insurrection.

Legal Interpretations

In contemporary legal contexts, insurrection has been defined and interpreted through legislation, court decisions, and scholarly analysis. Legal scholars and experts weigh various factors, including the intent of those involved, the scale and organization of the uprising, and the threat posed to the government's stability.

The Role of Intent

Intent plays a crucial role in determining whether an event constitutes insurrection. Did the individuals involved intend to overthrow the government or disrupt its operations? This question forms the crux of legal analysis in cases of alleged insurrection.

The 14th Amendment's Application

Considering these legal definitions and historical examples, the application of the 14th Amendment to the events of January 6th becomes a matter of scrutiny. Did the actions of the mob that breached the Capitol meet the legal threshold of insurrection as envisioned by the framers of the amendment?

As we delve deeper into the legal and political ramifications of January 6th and its potential impact on Donald Trump's presidential eligibility under the 14th Amendment, a fundamental understanding of insurrection—its historical context, legal definitions, and interpretations—will be paramount. The discussion surrounding whether the events of that day constituted insurrection or rebellion is central to the broader conversation about the Constitution's application in these unprecedented times.

Chapter 3: Legal Experts and Political Opinions

3.1 Debates among Legal Scholars

Regarding Donald Trump's ability to run for office, University of Baltimore law professor Kim Wehle posed a fascinating legal query in POLITICO Magazine at the beginning of last year: Considering his behavior in the days following the 2020 presidential election, may the 14th Amendment, which forbade former Confederates from running for office after the Civil War, also ban the former president from running again?

Now that Trump is facing his fourth criminal indictment, this one for attempting to rig the Georgia 2020 election, the notion is gathering support. William Baude of the University of Chicago and Michael Stokes Paulsen of the University of St. Thomas, two conservative legal experts connected to the Federalist Society, supported the thesis in the New York Times earlier this month. Two additional voices from opposing ideologies joined the chorus in a recent Atlantic article: Both former conservative judge J. Michael Luttig and liberal constitutional scholar Laurence Tribe at Harvard Law School agree that the Constitution stands between Trump and the White House. Asa Hutchinson, the former governor of Arkansas, brought it up during the first GOP debate this week, saying he would not "support somebody who's been convicted of a serious felony or who is disqualified under our Constitution."

They base their case on the 14th Amendment's Section 3, which prohibits former civilian or military officials from holding office if they "shall have engaged in insurrection or rebellion" against the federal government. Since the Reconstruction Era, the clause has largely been inactive. However, efforts to remove Trump from the ballot in important states have already begun as a result of his federal and state indictments in the uprising on January 6.

On January 6, 2021, Donald Trump, who was president at the time, addressed his supporters from The Ellipse near the White House.

It is questionable whether it is politically wise to exclude Trump from the presidential election using a constitutional provision, depriving voters of a free option regarding whether he should take office again. The issue of whether Section 3 "self-enacts" in his situation is also up for debate. Is he ineligible just because of what he did, or does he need to be found guilty?

Despite all of this, history indicates that the 14th Amendment's creators specifically had these threats in mind. They intended to remove from office anyone who made an effort to overturn the Constitution and bring an end to our form of government. It's important to explore the history of Section 3 in order to see why Trump might be ineligible to serve under the Constitution.

Republicans in Washington confronted a dual dilemma in the early post-Civil War period.

The Confederacy had been defeated, and they had forced the Southern states to stay in the Union. However, success could turn out to be a Trojan horse. Having their previous relationship with the federal government restored, Southern states may soon send senators and representatives to Congress, where they could work together with their Northern Democratic allies to take back control of the government and effectively turn the clock back to 1860. Even worse, the previous three-fifths agreement was rendered meaningless by the abolition of slavery. Even though Southern states made it clear early on that they intended to keep Black residents in a state of permanent political, social, and economic subjugation by passing "Black Codes" in the summer and fall of 1865 that severely limited the rights of free Black people, Southern representation in Congress and the electoral college would rise.

Even worse, Andrew Johnson became the presidency after Abraham Lincoln's death because, like other War Democrats, he backed the Union effort and advocated emancipation as a war measure and goal. Johnson now sought to quickly restore the old Union (but without slavery). Between the spring and December, when the new Congress would take office, Johnson took steps to recognize new, Democratic-controlled governments, first in North Carolina and then throughout the South. Johnson also issued a broad amnesty proclamation that pardoned all former Confederates except for 14 categories of people, the majority of whom were large landowners with property worth more than $20,000 (a lofty sum at the time) or high officials of the government. Even though, against the counsel of moderate Republicans who were otherwise inclined to believe him, Johnson started issuing a number of presidential pardons to these individuals throughout the fall.

Most Republicans were startled and horrified by these occurrences, especially radicals like Pennsylvania's Rep. Thaddeus Stevens, the stern, irascible "Dictator of the House." Stevens, who presided over the Ways and Means Committee throughout the war, was also the unofficial floor leader for the House Republican caucus thanks to his piercing gaze and brutal power. In his zeal to punish the South and enforce Black political and economic equality, he maintained strict control over the chamber even as he pushed for measures that were significantly more radical than those of his caucus. Stevens promoted the notion that the Southern states were "conquered territories," their inhabitants were no longer American citizens, and hence had no right to self-govern, much less take part in the governing of the entire country.

When the newly elected Congress, chosen in November 1864, gathered on Monday, December 4, the notion was put to the test for the first time. (Congressmen didn't take their seats until 13 months after the election in the 19th century.) The chamber was filled with several members-elect from Southern states, the majority of whom had served the Confederacy in military or civilian positions.

The New York Tribune noted that Stevens, who bore "his 70 years as though they were 40," bore his age with "his 70 years as though they were 40." The Clerk of the House, Edward McPherson, who was Stevens' protégé and himself a former Pennsylvania congressman, then began calling the roll. Horace Maynard of Tennessee, a Unionist who remained devoted to the United States, was among the members from the former Confederate states whose names he skipped over. "Mr. Clerk, I beg to say that in calling the roll of the members—" Maynard said as he stood up.

The chamber was told by McPherson through the sound of his gavel banging that "the Clerk will be compelled to object to any interruption of the call of the roll."

Does the clerk refuse to listen to me? Maynard begged.

He was ignored by McPherson, who made it clear that he did not regard members-elect from Confederate states as members proper by reminding the House that only members were allowed to present procedural motions. Stevens responded angrily when a Democrat raised the question of how Andrew Johnson, a Tennessean, could serve as president if his state was not a member of the union: "It is not essential. We all understand it. Johnson had been chosen to serve as vice president by the allied states in 1864, thus it didn't matter where he was from. After McPherson finished the roll, the Republican Party maintained its majority in Congress.

The 14th Amendment, which guarantees citizenship and equal rights to all people, Black or White, who were born in the U.S., was passed by Congress over the course of the following three years, putting the goals of Radical Reconstruction in writing. The Reconstruction Act, which was also passed by Congress, divided the South into military districts, mandated the ratification of the 14th Amendment by former Confederate states, and established new state governments that guaranteed Black men's equal access to the ballot box. They could only send delegates to Congress after being granted readmission to the United States.

At first, it was effective. Until those Reconstruction governments were overthrown one by one through a combination of paramilitary violence and election fraud, Republicans were able to ensure that former Confederate military and civilian officials were barred from holding office. Southern states also granted voting rights to their Black citizens, some of whom served in Congress. The benefits of Reconstruction, however, began to fade as the North lost interest in maintaining a military presence in the South and when Johnson issued a broad amnesty proclamation that applied to the majority of former Confederates.

Many former insurrectionists had returned to Congress by the middle of the 1870s. Alexander

Stephens, the former vice president of the Confederacy, was one of them.

The question of whether Section 3 is "self-enacting"—that is, if Donald Trump's actions disqualify him even in the absence of a conviction—is being debated among legal specialists. There is some, albeit less, debate over whether Section 3 was intended to provide a temporary threshold for eligibility to hold federal office rather than to apply broadly to former Confederates.

However, the 14th Amendment's background demonstrates its universal applicability. Confederate officials and office holders specifically conspired to rig an election, whether through violence or coercion. They attempted to destroy the United States by first leaving and then using force because they did not like the results of the 1860 election.

That was considered "insurrection or rebellion" against the US government, according to Section 3. It's difficult to argue that what happened in the aftermath of the 2020 election wasn't the same thing. On January 6, insurrectionists marched in unison with a previous generation of Americans who sought to overthrow our political system by carrying the Confederate battle flag into the Capitol. It doesn't make it any different that it was a botched attempt and that it didn't succeed.

3.2 Political Perspectives

A D.C.-based group and six Colorado voters have launched a lawsuit to remove former President Donald Trump from the ballot. The complaint adds its voice to a growing chorus of Democrats contending that Trump's alleged participation in the events of January 6, 2021, constitutes an "insurrection or rebellion," citing the 14th Amendment, which prohibits insurrectionists from holding public office.

It's absurd—ugly political campaigning of the kind that has become the standard in modern times as partisans attempt to influence our elections via the legal system. The 14th Amendment's wording, historical background, and legal implications all expose this attempt for what it is—the product of desperate Democrats hoping to create a political barrier to Trump's bid for the presidency in 2024.

The 14th Amendment's Section 3 states that anybody who "engages in insurrection or rebellion" is ineligible to hold any office. Although some think Trump's performance on January 6 matches this description, they are mistaken. The amendment's precise language makes direct reference to the uprising and rebellion of the Confederate states during the Civil War, and its goal was to prevent those who actively supported the cause from holding public office, not to act as a general rule that could be applied to candidates in the future based on arbitrary interpretation.

In reality, the absence of any established standards for evaluating whether someone is ineligible to run for office under the 14th Amendment is evidence that its application was meant to be limited. After all, there would be clear rules for recognizing and deciding such circumstances if it were intended to be a general norm.

The issue of standing is the next to be addressed. The 14th Amendment's disqualification language does not specifically provide a procedure for evaluating eligibility, which begs the issue of who would have the power to do so. Without a defined procedure, individual states or party organizations can theoretically rule that a candidate is ineligible based on their interpretation, which would result in uneven enforcement of the law.

Furthermore, it would be perilous to construe the 14th Amendment in a way that disqualifies candidates based on allegations of insurrection or revolt. Both political parties may use this broad interpretation to target undesirable candidates, further eroding trust and escalating political rifts.

Consider this: If Republicans can use the 14th Amendment to exclude Trump, what's to stop them from doing the same for anybody who supported or encouraged rioting in the wake of tragedies like the murder of George Floyd? This might stifle genuine political discourse and introduce an unprecedented amount of subjectivity into the voting process.

Also keep in mind that in the instance of President Trump, no charges of rebellion or insurrection have been brought against him.

Then there is the effect it would have on the due process rights of former President Trump. Although others contend that Trump should be disqualified even in the absence of a criminal record, it is important to defend everyone's basic rights, even presidential candidates. Disqualifying a candidate without a conviction would violate the rule of assumed innocence and deny voters the opportunity to choose the candidate of their choice.

The case against disqualifying Trump based on the 14th Amendment is further supported by historical precedents and legal interpretations. Reiterating the argument that the disqualification clause exclusively targeted the Confederate cause, Congress approved amnesty acts in 1872 and 1898 that essentially invalidated the effect of the Disqualifications Clause for Americans who would have been disqualified under Section 3.

In addition, courts have determined that the Disqualifications Clause does not operate automatically, thus Congress must pass explicit legislation to define the procedure for excluding someone from Section 3 of the Constitution. Since there is currently no equivalent law, the amendment's narrow reach and intended purpose are further highlighted.

When arguing against Trump's eligibility, critics often use a biased and political interpretation of the 14th Amendment. While some support a strict reading of the amendment's Equal Protection Clause, restricting its applicability to those who were formerly slaves and their descendants, others support a wide and liberal view of the disqualification clause. The reasons for applying several provisions of the same amendment in different ways are unclear in light of this contradiction.

3.3 Public Reactions

In a pending court dispute over whether he should be allowed to vote in 2024, Donald Trump is chiming in.

Trump has denied any wrongdoing, but an increasing number of conservative academics have brought up the constitutional claim that his attempts to annul the results of the 2020 election exclude him from ever holding public office again.

From Texas to Alabama to Trump, this is everything you should know from the campaign road.

Trump rejects the 14th Amendment challenge to his eligibility
Arguments that Section 3 of the 14th Amendment may be used to oust the previous president from office in 2024 are being rebuffed by the former president.

On Monday night, he said in a fresh social media post that "almost all legal scholars have voiced opinions that the 14th Amendment has no legal basis or standing relative to the upcoming 2024 Presidential Election."

Conservative academics, such as William Baude, Michael Stokes Paulsen, and former federal judge J. Michael Luttig—all members of the conservative Federalist Society—suggest the opposite. Laurence Tribe, an emeritus professor of law at Harvard, joined Luttig in arguing the position.

This section of the 14th Amendment states that a public official is not permitted to hold public office if they took an oath to support the Constitution while they were in office but later "engaged in insurrection or rebellion against the same, or [gave] aid or comfort to the enemies thereof," unless they are granted amnesty by a two-thirds vote of Congress. The crux of this argument is how Trump's actions after the 2020 election and before January 6 relate to this provision.

In his new position, Trump referred to any such 14th Amendment-related legal challenges as "election interference."

The 14th Amendment movement against Trump has gaining momentum in a number of states, including key swing states like Arizona, Michigan, and New Hampshire. Similar attempts against past Republicans have fallen short.

Trump's hold on his party is still strong despite historical legal issues, according to a new poll
No president has ever been impeached twice, much alone four times, or been charged with a crime. He has characterized all of these allegations as political retaliation and entered not guilty pleas to all of his charges in Florida, Georgia, New York, and Washington, D.C.

However, a recent CNN poll reveals that Trump continues to have enormous support from the GOP base, who will decide who their party's candidate for president will be. Polls from ABC News and Ipsos indicated that Trump had some difficulties with the public's perception of his rising criminal accusations while running for the presidency again.

He is still in front of the 2024 Republican field, polling more than 30 points higher than his closest rival, Florida Governor Ron DeSantis: 52% to 18%, according to a recent SSRS survey for CNN.

Approximately 43% of GOP-aligned voters who were polled between August 25 and August 31, the typical Labor Day start to the election cycle, claimed they were unwavering supporters of Donald Trump, while 20% said they were solidly behind another candidate and 37% said they had no preference or would change their mind.

Paxton appears in court

Suspended Texas Attorney General Ken Paxton's impeachment trial, which is anticipated to last several weeks, started on Tuesday morning at the state Capitol in Austin. He will soon discover his destiny.

A bipartisan group of Texas House managers has accused the state's top attorney, Paxton, of abuse of power despite his lengthy history of avoiding prior problems.

In the event that he is found guilty, Republican Paxton may be forever disqualified from holding another public office in his state.

Paxton has refuted all accusations of impropriety and called the impeachment process a "sham."

The trial might have an impact on one of the largest states in the nation, which is traditionally a stronghold of the Republican Party but has been shifting more and more Democratic in recent elections.

"I think that effort to focus or at least see Texas as a possibility operates apart from Paxton's corruption and the effort to remove him," said Matt Angle, director of the Lone Star Project, a Democratic research and political organization, to ABC News. "But it certainly helps."

After Alabama failed to include a district for Black voters, the court mandates a new map.
The newly revised congressional district lines in Alabama were unanimously overturned on Tuesday by a three-judge panel. The judges determined that the GOP-backed plan did not adhere to the Voting Rights Act because it did not provide a second district where Black voters would probably be able to elect their chosen candidate.

A new map for the 2024 elections will be created by specialists designated by the court.

Alabama is anticipated to appeal the ruling to the Supreme Court of the United States.

Alabama's layout was first invalidated by a federal court decision in 2022, which mandated that the legislature create "two districts in which Black voters either comprise a voting-age majority or something quite close to it."

However, the group said on Tuesday that they were "deeply troubled" that Alabama legislators will pass a plan in 2022 that would reject their recommendations.

The congressional boundaries for Alabama might affect the chances of winning control of the U.S. House of Representatives in 2024. Only five seats put Republicans in control of the legislature, although Black people in Alabama often support Democrats.

Chapter 4: The Supreme Court's Role

According to distinguished former federal judge Michael Luttig, the US Supreme Court will probably soon decide whether Donald Trump is qualified to run for president in 2024.

According to several legal professionals, Trump could be ineligible for office under the 14th Amendment's section 3. The law states that if a person has "previously taken an oath... to support the constitution" and then "engaged in insurrection or rebellion against the same," they are unable to occupy federal office. By interpreting that text, Luttig and several other well-known conservative academics have concluded that Trump is ineligible to run for president due to his acts on January 6 and his attempts to rig the 2020 election.

Democrat leader calls it a "powerful argument" Trump is ineligible under the 14th Amendment, according to some historians, who also doubt if Trump's actions genuinely constituted an uprising.

The particular procedure for doing so is unknown, and the clause has never been put into action. Secretaries of state, who are responsible for monitoring candidate eligibility standards, are analyzing how the procedure is likely to go.

During an interview on MSNBC's Velshi on Sunday, Luttig said, "This is one of the most fundamental questions that could ever be decided under our constitution." And the United States Supreme Court will decide on it sooner rather than later, and probably before the first primaries.

The current Supreme Court has a 6-3 conservative supermajority, and three of the justices were selected by Trump. It will likely come to the court at a time when criticism of the institution is mounting due to several ethical scandals and its controversial decision to reverse Roe v. Wade last year.

Election authorities in some of the states with the earliest primaries would likely need to decide shortly how to handle challenges to Trump's eligibility that several organizations have vowed to launch. The Republican secretary of state in New Hampshire, Dave Scanlan, told NBC News that his office had received a flood of calls from Trump supporters after conservative radio host Charlie Kirk falsely claimed that Scanlan was attempting to remove Trump from the ballot. They are likely to face tremendous pressure.

In a joint statement with John Formella, the attorney general of New Hampshire, Scanlan stated that "neither the secretary of state's office nor the attorney general's office has taken any position regarding the potential applicability of section three of the 14th amendment to the United States Constitution to the upcoming presidential election cycle." The attorney general's office has been asked by the secretary of state's office to advise the secretary of state on the interpretation of section three of the 14th amendment to the US Constitution and whether

or not it would be relevant to the forthcoming
presidential elect
ion cycle.

Chapter 5: The Role of Key State Officials

5.1 Perspectives of State Secretaries of State

Liberal organizations and legal experts assert that former President Donald Trump is unable to be president after the assault on the U.S. Capitol on January 6, 2021, despite the fact that he is now leading the Republican primary.

Anyone who ever swore an oath to defend the Constitution but thereafter "engaged" in "insurrection or rebellion" against it is prohibited from holding public office under the 14th Amendment. The post-Civil War clause, according to an increasing number of legal experts, applies to Trump because of his participation in attempting to rig the 2020 presidential election and motivating his supporters to attack the U.S. Capitol.

Should state election officials put Trump on the ballot over these concerns, two leftist charities have threatened legal action.

The initiative is probably going to start a string of litigation and appeals across numerous states that will finally end up before the US Supreme Court, maybe during the 2024 presidential primary season. The situation further complicates the already turbulent nominating process caused by the front-runner's involvement in four criminal proceedings.

Now that Republicans are expected to begin selecting their candidate, beginning with the Iowa caucuses on January 15, Trump's very eligibility to run might be contested.

Gerard Magliocca, an Indiana University law professor, cautioned that there is a "very real prospect" that these lawsuits would be active throughout the primaries and that different results may occur in other states prior to the Supreme Court's ultimate ruling. Imagine that you believe he is ineligible, but there is an other primary where he is on the ballot.

A newly published law review paper by two renowned conservative legal professors, William Baude and Michael Paulsen, has given the subject more attention even though the majority of litigation is unlikely to start until October, when states start setting their ballots for the forthcoming primary. They came to the conclusion that the provision in the third part of the 14th Amendment required Trump to be disqualified from voting.

Anyone who previously swore an oath to uphold the Constitution and "has engaged in insurrection or rebellion against the same, or given aid or comfort to the enemies thereof" is prohibited from serving in Congress, the military, or holding federal or state posts.

According to Baude and Paulsen's essay, which will appear in the University of Pennsylvania Law Review, the meaning is obvious.

They add that "taking Section Three seriously means excluding from present or future office those who sought to thwart lawful government authority under the Constitution in the wake of the 2020 election."

Asa Hutchinson, a former governor of Arkansas, brought up the subject at last week's Republican presidential debate in Milwaukee and cautioned that "this is something that could disqualify him under our rules and under the Constitution."

The group Free Speech For People wrote to the chief election officer in each of the 50 states in 2021 to demand that Trump be fired if he were to run for president again. Ron Fein, the group's legal director, said that after years of quiet, authorities are now talking about the issue.

The 14th Amendment's authors "learned the bloody lesson that an oath-breaking insurrectionist can't be trusted to return to power once they engage in insurrection," Fein added.

Prior to the 2022 midterm elections, the organization filed a lawsuit to have Republican U.S. Representative Marjorie Taylor-Greene and then-Rep. Madison Cawthorn disqualified from running due to their support for the Jan. 6 protest. Greene's lawsuit was heard by a court who decided in her favor; Cawthorn's petition was dismissed since he lost his primary.

The intricate legal difficulties were brought to light on Wednesday when the Arizona Republic reported that Secretary of State Adrian Fontes said he was unable to remove anybody off Arizona's presidential ballot due to a state high court decision that only Congress had the authority to do so. In an interview with the Republic, Fontes, a Democrat, referred to the decision as "dead, flat wrong" but said that he would follow it anyway.

Trump's opponents may still file a lawsuit in federal court to get him removed off the ballot if he appears on the Arizona ballot.

The legal quagmire is being cautiously navigated by other secretaries of state.

Jocelyn Benson, the Democrat who serves as Michigan's secretary of state, said earlier this week in a radio interview that "there are valid legal arguments being made" to keep Donald Trump off the ballot and that she is addressing the issue with other secretaries of state, including those in key presidential battleground states.

WHO ELSE IS INCLUDED IN TRUMP'S INDICTION IN THE GEORGIA ELECTION CASE?

The Republican secretary of state in Georgia who defied demands from President Trump to reverse the state's 2020 election results, Brad Raffensperger, indicated that voters should decide the matter.

In a statement sent through email, he said, "I have been clear that voters are knowledgeable and deserve the right to determine elections.

Trump claims that any attempt to keep him off a state's ballot constitutes "election interference"; this is how he is defining the criminal charges brought against him in New York and Atlanta as well as the federal accusations brought against him by prosecutors in Washington, D.C., and Florida.

According to Trump, "And I think what's happening is that there's really been a backlash against it," he said in an interview with Newsmax, a conservative station.

According to spokesperson Anna Sventek, the New Hampshire secretary of state's office received a ton of communications regarding the problem on Monday. A conservative celebrity had wrongly stated earlier in the day that the state was preparing to remove Trump's name off the ballot.

John Anthony Castro, a distant Republican presidential contender from Texas, complained in a New Hampshire court on Wednesday, claiming that the 14th Amendment disqualified Trump from being on the state's ballot.

It is anticipated that the eventual, larger judicial challenges would attract more legal clout. The case is not a lock, according to Michael McConnell, a conservative Stanford University law professor who does not endorse Trump.

McConnell challenges whether the clause even applies to the presidency given that it is not one of the positions directly mentioned in the 14th Amendment, which instead refers to the "elector of president and vice president." He said that it's unclear from a legal standpoint whether the Jan. 6 assault counts as a "insurrection" or is merely a less serious occurrence like a riot.

But if Trump is finally removed off any state ballot, McConnell is equally concerned about the political precedent that will be set.

"Trump is not the only issue. "Their opponents are going to run in and try to get them disqualified in every election where someone says something supportive of a riot that impedes the enforcement of laws," he warned.

The 14th Amendment, which was ratified in 1868, helped safeguard civil rights for freed slaves and, ultimately, for all Americans. It was also used to stop former Confederate leaders from running for office and seizing control of the government they had just overthrown.

The provision enables Congress to revoke the prohibition, which it did in 1872 when public support for maintaining the ban waned. After then, the clause was nearly never used. A socialist was denied a seat in Congress in 1919 because Congress believed he had supported the nation's enemies during World War I. A New

Mexico court disqualified a rural county commissioner who had arrived in the Capitol on January 6 from office last year, marking the first time the clause had been used since then.

Trump's reelection campaign is anticipated to file a lawsuit, perhaps carrying the matter all the way to the US Supreme Court, if any state forbids him from running. Free Speech For People and another group, Citizens for Responsibility and Ethics in Washington, would probably contest his inclusion on the ballot if no state forbade him.

Before the general election, the high court must decide the case, according to Edward Foley, an Ohio State University law professor. His concern is that if the issue of Trump's eligibility is not settled and he wins, Democrats would attempt to prevent his inauguration on January 6, 2025, sparking another democratic crisis.

Those advocating the use of the amendment concur and assert that they believe the situation is obvious.

"This is not a penalty. As Noah Bookbinder, head of Citizens for Responsibility and Ethics in Washington, put it, "it's like saying a president needs to be 35 years old and a natural born citizen." Additionally, you must not have assisted in planning an insurrection against the government.

Conclusion: The Legacy of the 14th Amendment's Application

Passed by Congress June 13, 1866, and ratified July 9, 1868, the 14th Amendment extended liberties and rights granted by the Bill of Rights to formerly enslaved people.

Following the Civil War, Congress submitted to the states three amendments as part of its Reconstruction program to guarantee equal civil and legal rights to Black citizens. A major provision of the 14th Amendment was to grant citizenship to "All persons born or naturalized in the United States," thereby granting citizenship to formerly enslaved people.

Another equally important provision was the statement that "nor shall any state deprive any person of life, liberty, or property, without due process of law; nor deny to any person within its jurisdiction the equal protection of the laws." The right to due process of law and equal protection of the law now applied to both the federal and state governments.

On June 16, 1866, the House Joint Resolution proposing the 14th Amendment to the Constitution was submitted to the states. On July 28, 1868, the 14th amendment was declared, in a certificate of the Secretary of State, ratified by the necessary 28 of the 37 States, and became part of the supreme law of the land.

Congressman John A. Bingham of Ohio, the primary author of the first section of the 14th Amendment, intended that the amendment also nationalize the Bill of Rights by making it binding upon the states. When introducing the amendment, Senator Jacob Howard of Michigan specifically stated that the privileges and immunities clause would extend to the states "the personal rights guaranteed and secured by the first eight amendments." Historians disagree on how widely Bingham's and Howard's views were shared at the time in the Congress, or across the country in general. No one in

Congress explicitly contradicted their view of the amendment, but only a few members said anything at all about its meaning on this issue. For many years, the Supreme Court ruled that the amendment did not extend the Bill of Rights to the states.

Not only did the 14th Amendment fail to extend the Bill of Rights to the states; it also failed to protect the rights of Black citizens. A legacy of Reconstruction was the determined struggle of Black and white citizens to make the promise of the 14th Amendment a reality. Citizens petitioned and initiated court cases, Congress enacted legislation, and the executive branch attempted to enforce measures that would guard all citizens' rights. While these citizens did not succeed in empowering the 14th Amendment during Reconstruction, they effectively articulated arguments and offered dissenting opinions that would be the basis for change in the 20th century.

Section 1.

All persons born or naturalized in the United States, and subject to the jurisdiction thereof, are citizens of the United States and of the State wherein they reside. No State shall make or enforce any law which shall abridge the privileges or immunities of citizens of the United States; nor shall any State deprive any person of life, liberty, or property, without due process of law; nor deny to any person within its jurisdiction the equal protection of the laws.

Section 2.

Representatives shall be apportioned among the several States according to their respective numbers, counting the whole number of persons in each State, excluding Indians not taxed. But when the right to vote at any election for the choice of electors for President and Vice-President of the United States, Representatives in Congress, the Executive and Judicial officers of a State, or the members of the Legislature thereof, is denied to any of the male inhabitants of such State, being twenty-one years of age, and citizens of the United States, or in any way abridged, except for participation in rebellion, or other crime, the basis of representation therein shall be reduced in the proportion which the number of such male citizens shall bear to the whole number of male citizens twenty-one years of age in such State.

Section 3.

No person shall be a Senator or Representative in Congress, or elector of President and Vice-President, or hold any office, civil or military, under the United States, or under any State, who, having previously taken an oath, as a member of Congress, or as an officer of the United States, or as a member of any State legislature, or as an executive or judicial officer of any State, to support the Constitution of the United States, shall have engaged in insurrection or rebellion against the same, or given aid or comfort to the enemies thereof. But Congress may by a vote of two-thirds of each House, remove such disability.

Section 4.

The validity of the public debt of the United States, authorized by law, including debts incurred for payment of pensions and bounties for services in suppressing insurrection or rebellion, shall not be questioned. But neither the United States nor any State shall assume or pay any debt or obligation incurred in aid of insurrection or rebellion against the United States, or any claim for the loss or emancipation of any slave; but all such debts, obligations and claims shall be held illegal and void.

Section 5.

The Congress shall have the power to enforce, by appropriate legislation, the provisions of this article.

www.ingramcontent.com/pod-product-compliance
Lightning Source LLC
Chambersburg PA
CBHW050844260726

48660CB00006B/2424